Christian Life Community and the Spirit of "Fratelli Tutti". On Fraternity and Social Friendship

Tarcisius Mukuka

Bibliographic information published by the German National Library:

The German National Library lists this publication in the National Bibliography; detailed bibliographic data are available on the Internet at http://dnb.dnb.de.

ISBN: 9783346317445
This book is also available as an ebook.

© GRIN Publishing GmbH
Nymphenburger Straße 86
80636 München

Print and binding: Books on Demand GmbH, Norderstedt, Germany
Printed on acid-free paper from responsible sources.

The present work has been carefully prepared. Nevertheless, authors and publishers do not incur liability for the correctness of information, notes, links and advice as well as any printing errors.

GRIN web shop: https://www.grin.com/document/965277

On Fraternity and Social Friendship
Christian Life Community [CLC] and the Spirit of *Fratelli Tutti*
A Paper delivered by
Dr Tarcisius Mukuka
To the St Ignatius Christian Life Community in Lusaka via Zoom
On Sunday, 29 November 2020

As I was writing this letter, the Covid-19 pandemic unexpectedly erupted, exposing our false securities. Aside from the different ways that various countries responded to the crisis, their inability to work together became quite evident. For all our hyper-connectivity, we witnessed a fragmentation that made it more difficult to resolve problems that affect us all. Anyone who thinks that the only lesson to be learned was the need to improve what we were already doing, or to refine existing systems and regulations, is denying reality. It is my desire that, in this our time, by acknowledging the dignity of each human person, we can contribute to the rebirth of a universal aspiration to fraternity (Pope Francis, *Fratelli Tutti* 2020: par 7–8).

1. Introduction

My thanks to Josephine Shamwana-Lungu for inviting me to share some thoughts on the recent encyclical by Pope Francis and to you all for joining us via Zoom. Jo and I have known each other as early as 1983. About a month ago, she and I were talking over the phone enthusing about Pope Francis' new encyclical. At that time, some priests did not even know there was a new encyclical. She told me how excited she was to be reading the new encyclical. At some point she used the phrase, "The Spirit of *Fratelli Tutti*" which I have incorporated in the title of my paper. It occurs to me that for members of Christian Life Community who wish to understand "The Spirit of *Fratelli Tutti*," they need not look further than CLC. It's there. This is my main point for our discussion this afternoon: namely, to ask, how can CLC help us to live out the Spirit of *Fratelli Tutti*? I am excited to be sharing that "Spirit of *Fratelli Tutti*" with the oldest CLC in Zambia with its impressive innings of over 30 years longevity.

I suggest that the Spirit of *Fratelli Tutti* is what we used to call *Ubwananyina* [siblings of the same mother] or as the Southern Africans would say, *Ubuntu*, captured in the saying, *Umuntu ngu muntu nga bantu* [a person is a person in and through other persons]. As my friend and erstwhile colleague Hugo Hinfelaar pointed out, "the *Bemba* term used to translate the concept of Humanism was the traditional expression: *ubwananyina*. This stressed the people's equality stemming from a common brotherhood and sisterhood as children of the same mothers and descended from the same ancestress" (Hinfelaar 1992: 151). This is the Spirit of *Fratelli Tutti* and this is how I propose to proceed. First, I will give a brief summary of the ethos of CLC as I was able to garner from its website. Any lacunae, I am happy for you to fill in. Second, I will explain what an encyclical is and why it is important. Third, I will give a whistle-stop tour of the eight chapters of the encyclical. Fourth, I hope to share as briefly as I can the reception of *Fratelli Tutti* so far. Fifth, I want to ask how *Fratelli Tutti* is challenging us as members of CLC and in my conclusion I hope to make some suggestions for the afterlife of *Fratelli Tutti*. Whether I shall manage to do this in the 15 minutes at my disposal remains to be seen.

2. A Brief Summary of the Ethos of CLC

According to the CLC website, the Christian Life Community is a global association of Christians, men and women, adults and young people, of all social conditions, who, inspired by the life and teaching of St Ignatius of Loyola want to be disciples of Jesus Christ more closely and work with Him by realising the Kingdom of God — a kingdom of peace, love and justice. The genius of CLC was to intuit long before Small Christian Communities that "small is beautiful" by having members make up small groups but these small groups or cells are not insular. They form part of larger communities organised regionally and nationally, all forming one World Community. That is why the CLC is present in all five continents, in more than sixty countries. As for its Ignatian ethos, I will let the website speak for itself. The spirituality is uncannily like *Fratelli Tutti*.

The charism and spirituality of CLC are Ignatian. Thus, the Spiritual Exercises of St Ignatius are both the specific source of our charism and the characteristic instrument of CLC spirituality. The CLC way of life is shaped by the features of Ignatian Christology: austere and simple, in solidarity with the poor and the outcasts of society, integrating contemplation and action, in all things living lives of love and service within the Church, always in a spirit of discernment.[1]

I will let Manuel Martínez Arteaga, the Uruguayan Executive Secretary of CLC describe that spirit which, as my friend Josephine Shamwana-Lungu says, encapsulates "The spirit of *Fratelli Tutti*." Writing in *Progressio* Manuel Martínez Arteaga reminds us. "Now, let's talk about the latest embrace in these recent times. It is a type of embrace which takes on many forms, but which shares a common feature: it is a virtual or spiritual hug. Many of our national communities are living through the effects of the Covid-19 epidemic. Many of us have had to celebrate our World CLC Day on March 25 through the celebrations of the Eucharist on social networks. These community meetings are happening through different internet platforms, often through methods that we are not accustomed to using. However, this is a time that has awakened in us our creativity, our drive for community, our desire to be present and take care of each other, even at a distance. It has become a time to rediscover the important things inside our hearts, and to realise that despite the individual circumstances which we are all experiencing, we can all fill our days with deep meaning, and with a prayer that carries trust and hope: We shall embrace again."[2]

3. A Papal Encyclical and Why it is Important

An encyclical is a long circular letter from the Pope sent to the bishops, priests and deacons (the three-fold ministry), consecrated persons and the Lay Faithful of the Roman Catholic Church in which an important theme regarding a pressing contemporary issue is addressed. The title of the encyclical is from the first two Latin words known as the incipit. The term comes from Latin, the official language of the Catholic Church, *encyclius*, that which goes round. The Latin is incidentally the root of our word encyclopaedia. This encyclical is then shared with the people of God at the national and diocesan level. It is a theological document and its language is not always easily digestible for the non-initiate or those who are not theologically literate at least up to undergraduate level. This is a big challenge to most, if not all, the ordinary Christians in the pew for whom theological matters are the equivalent of celestial higher mathematics.

Pope Francis has written three encyclicals. The first was *Lumen fidei* (The light of faith), which was released in 2013. *Lumen fidei* was largely the work of Francis' predecessor Benedict XVI. It is the first encyclical in the history of the Catholic Church written by two Popes, begun by Pope Benedict XVI and finished by Pope Francis. *Lumen fidei* is about the Christian faith as the guiding light that inspires social action as well as devotion to God, and illuminating every aspect of human existence. *Laudato si'* (English: May you be praised) is the second encyclical of Pope Francis. The encyclical has the subtitle "on care for our common home." In it, the Pope takes a swing at consumerism and unbridled development, laments environmental degradation and global warming, and calls all people of the world to take "swift and unified global action." When it was officially released at noon on 18 June 2015, I was part of a task force put together by St Mary's University to come up with a theological appreciation of the encyclical. Because of the media embargo, I only managed to get an advance copy the night before which had been released to the press and only available in Italian. I worked with this copy through the night so that our theological statement could coincide with the official launching at midday Rome time and 11.00 hours UK time. On Saturday, 5 September 2020, the Vatican Press Office announced a third encyclical for Pope Francis. This third encyclical is entitled *Fratelli tutti*, which means "Brothers all" in Italian, focusing on the theme of human fraternity and social friendship, according to the Holy See Press Office.

At the time the announcement was made, I hoped that by the time it was published, the title of the encyclical would be adjusted to "*Fratelli e Sorelle tutti*" [Brothers and sisters all] but given the justification given by Andrea Tornielli, I doubted whether that would be forthcoming. This is how the announcement was made, "*Nel pomeriggio di Sabato 3 ottobre 2020 il Santo Padre Francesco si recherà ad Assisi per firmare la nuova Enciclica 'Fratelli tutti' sulla fraternità e l'amicizia sociale*" [In the afternoon of Saturday 3 October 2020, the Holy Father Francis will travel to Assisi to sign the new encyclical 'All Brothers' on fraternity and social friendship].[3] The title of the new encyclical comes from the writings of St. Francis of Assisi, the namesake of Pope Francis. The specific line in question comes from *Admonition VI*, one of twenty-eight exhortations or mini-homilies that St. Francis delivered to his brother friars. Typically, these short texts offer a practical reflection on some passage from Scripture. *Admonition VI* begins, "Let all of us, brothers, consider the Good Shepherd Who bore the suffering of the cross to save His sheep"[4] [*Attendamus, omnes fratres, bonum pastorem, qui pro ovibus suis salvandis crucis sustinuit passionem*].[5] In defence of St Francis, the admonition was addressed to his "brothers" [*fratres*]. He could hardly be accused of gender bias and in using the admonition as the incipit of his encyclical, Pope Francis is just quoting *verbatim*. As is now well known, the third encyclical was published on 4 October 2020.

4. A Whistle-Stop Tour of the Eight Chapters of *Fratelli Tutti*

The encyclical is divided into 8 chapters and the subtitles will suffice to give us a flavour of this new social encyclical, with Spanish subtitles in square brackets: Introduction (par 1–8), Chapter 1: Dark clouds cover the world (par 9–55) [*Las Sombras de un Mundo Cerrado*], Chapter 2: A stranger on the road (par 56–86) [*Un Extraño en el Camino*], Chapter 3: Envisaging and engendering an open world (par 87–127) [*Pensar y Gestar un Mundo Abierto*], Chapter 4: A heart open to the world (par 128–153) [*Un Corazón Abierto al Mundo Entero*], Chapter 5: A better kind of politics (par 154–197) [*La Mejor Política*], Chapter 6: Dialogue and friendship in society (par 198–224) [*Diálogo y Amistad Social*], Chapter 7: Paths of renewed encounter (par 225–270) [*Caminos de Reencuentro*] and Chapter 8: Religions at the service of fraternity in our world (271–287) [*Las Religiones al Servicio de la Fraternidad en el Mundo*].[6] Given the convergence of themes, it would be remiss if I did not give a brief summary of the chapters of *Fratelli Tutti* mentioned above.

i. **Chapter 1**, "Dark Clouds over a Closed World," of the encyclical paints a picture replete with manipulation and misunderstanding of concepts such as democracy, freedom, justice; the loss of meaning of social community and history; selfishness and indifference toward the common good; the prevalence of a market logic based on profit and the culture of waste; unemployment, racism, poverty; the disparity of rights and its aberrations such as slavery, trafficking, women subjugated and then forced to abort, organ trafficking etc. Quite clearly, this is a lethal cocktail of a dysfunctional world requiring drastic solutions. In the context of a post Covid-19 era, there cannot be any return to business as usual.

ii. **Chapter 2**, "A stranger on the road" is dedicated to the famous figure of the Good Samaritan (Luke 10.25–37). In it, the Pope emphasises that in an unhealthy society such as ours — what Peter Morrall has referred to as "Insane Society" (Morrall 2020) — that turns its back on suffering and is "illiterate" in caring for the frail and vulnerable needs to be converted and practice what St Paul calls *agathōsýnē*[7] in Gal 5.22 — meaning inherently good, intrinsic goodness (especially as a unique quality and condition); as relating to believers, the goodness that comes from God and showing itself in spiritual, moral excellence. Chapter 2 reminds us that we are in an era in which "we are all called to become neighbours to others by overcoming prejudices, personal interests, historic and cultural barriers." For the Pope, just as for the new Instruction from the *Congregation for the Clergy*, "Pastoral conversion of the parish community in the service of the evangelising mission of the Church" we are co-responsible in creating a society that is inclusive, integrative and uplifting "those who have fallen" by the wayside or are suffering. Such acts of love build bridges because "we were made for love" (*Fratelli Tutti* 2020: par 88).

iii. **Chapter 3**, "Envisaging and engendering an open world," Pope Francis exhorts us to go "outside the self" — to be missionary — in order to find "a fuller existence in another" (*Ibid*), opening ourselves up to the other according to the dynamism of charity which makes us tend toward "universal fulfilment" (*Fratelli Tutti* 2020: par 95). This call to an open world is made in the light of the plight of migrants forced to flee war-torn areas such as Syria or simply migrants, in South America, fleeing brutal dictatorships. Their efforts are often met by countries closed to migrants. Countries, such as the United Kingdom, once marked by the commonwealth spirit of openness are now become insular.

iv. **Chapter 4**, entitled "A heart open to the whole world" and focuses on those fleeing from war, persecution, natural catastrophes, unscrupulous trafficking, and those who are ripped from their communities of origin. This chapter spells out the principles of chapter 3 driven by the dynamism of charity. The Pope reiterates the constant message of his pontificate epitomised in the ministry of his Almoner, Cardinal Konrad Krajewski that migrants are to be welcomed, protected, supported and integrated. But the Pope introduces an important caveat that unnecessary migration — mainly and purely for economic advancement — needs to be avoided by creating concrete opportunities to live in dignity in the countries of origin.

v.   **Chapter 5**, "A better kind of politics" represents one of the most valuable expressions of charity because it is placed at the service of the common good (*Fratelli Tutti* 2020: par 180) and recognises the importance of people, understood as an open category, available for discussion and dialogue (*Fratelli Tutti* 2020: par 160). This is the populism indicated by Francis, which counters that "populism" which ignores the legitimacy of the notion of "people" by attracting consensuses in order to exploit them for its own service and fomenting selfishness in order to increase its own popularity (*Fratelli Tutti* 2020: par 159). But a better politics is also one that protects work, an "essential dimension of social life" (*Fratelli Tutti* 2020: par 162). In Zambia, in the light of the 2021 General Elections, we are in dire need of "a better kind of politics." The Church in Zambia can help the nation to spell out what "a better kind of politics" might look like by election time in 2021 — a better kind of politics that disavows *ochlocracy* or mob rule, the rule of government by a mass of unruly, uncouth and unelected people and the intimidation of the citizenry by largely illiterate party cadres at the behest of the head of state who is effectively the Cadre-in-Chief.

vi.   **Chapter 6**, "Dialogue and friendship in society" is for me, the *pièce de résistance* of *Fratelli Tutti*, given that my predilection for Scripture should have led me to chapter 2. The chapter proposes solutions to the dreary picture painted in chapter one. The Pope proposes the concept of life as the "art of encounter" (*Fratelli Tutti* 2020: par 215), quoting Vinicius de Moraes' *Samba da Benção*, from the recording *Um encontro no Au bon Gourmet*, Rio de Janeiro (2 August 1962). Marcus Vinícius da Cruz e Mello Moraes (19 October 1913 – 9 July 1980), to give him his full set names. He was nicknamed *O Poetinha* (The little poet), was a Brazilian poet, lyricist, essayist and playwright. Along with frequent collaborator Antônio Carlos Jobim, his lyrics and compositions were part of the birth of *bossa nova* [new trend or new wave] music. He recorded several albums and also served as a diplomat. The Pope is indebted to him for the use of the phrase "Life, for all its confrontations, is the art of encounter" [Portuguese: *A vida é a arte do encontro, embora haja tanto desencontro na vida*] cited in the encyclical (*Fratelli Tutti* 2020: par 215). There is an intended pun on "encounter" [*encontro*] and "confrontations" [*desencontro*] lost in translation. It is maintained in the Spanish original as is to be expected, *encuentro* and *desencuentro*. For the Pope, this is an encounter with everyone, even with those on the world's peripheries and with original peoples, because "each of us can learn something from others. No one is useless and no one is expendable" (*Fratelli Tutti* 2020: par 215). Then, of particular note, is the Pope's reference to the miracle of "kindness." The Spanish word translated as "kindness" is "*amabilidad*" while the French has "*bienveillance*." A better English translation of "*amabilidad*" is amiability. The French "*bienveillance*" meaning benevolence, is closer to the intended significance of *amabilidad* than kindness. In the words of the encyclical, this is an attitude to be recovered because it is a star "shining in the midst of darkness" and "frees us from the cruelty that at times infects human relationships, from the anxiety that prevents us from thinking of others, from the frantic flurry of activity that forgets that others also have a right to be happy" in the contemporary era (*Fratelli Tutti* 2020: par 222–224).

vii.   **Chapter 7**, "Paths of Renewed Encounter," reiterates the value and promotion of peace by underscoring that peace is connected to truth, justice and mercy. Far from the desire for vengeance, it is "proactive" and aims at forming a society based on service to others and on the pursuit of reconciliation and mutual development (*Fratelli Tutti* 2020: par 227–229) citing the example of the Truth and Reconciliation Commission of South Africa (cf. Fratelli Tutti 2020: par 229). Thus, peace is an "art" that involves and regards everyone and in which each one must do his or her part in "a never-ending task" (*Fratelli Tutti* 2020: par 232). Forgiveness is linked to peace: we must love everyone, without exception.

viii.   **Chapter 8**, "Religions at the service of fraternity in our world," emphasizes that terrorism is not due to religion but to erroneous interpretations of religious texts, as well as "policies linked to hunger, poverty, injustice, oppression" (*Fratelli Tutti* 2020: par 282–283). This journey of peace among religions is possible and that it is therefore necessary to guarantee religious freedom, a fundamental human right for all believers (*Fratelli Tutti* 2020: par 279). Critics, no doubt, will cite the fate of the underground Church in China as a case in point. In the context of the conversion of the parish community in the service of the evangelising mission of the Church, Catholic parishes and dioceses that are converted would greatly contribute to the new world order being proposed by the new encyclical. The Pope, for his part quotes the Grand Imam Ahmad Al-Tayyeb, 5 times in the encyclical, together with whom they declared "that religions must never incite war, hateful attitudes, hostility and extremism, nor must they incite violence or the shedding of blood. These tragic realities are the consequence of a deviation from religious teachings. They result from a political manipulation of religions and from interpretations made by religious groups who, in the course of history, have taken advantage of the power of religious sentiment in the hearts of men and women... God, the Almighty, has no need to be defended by anyone and does not want his name to be used to terrorise people" (*Fratelli Tutti* 2020: par 285). The Pope was citing from the "Document on Human Fraternity for World Peace and Living Together."[8] Michael Sean Winters rightly asks, "If this pandemic does not shake us out of our post-modern cultural and moral and spiritual lethargy, what will? Pope Francis is throwing the Catholic Church and the whole world a lifeline. Will we grab it?"[9]

After this blistering whistle-stop tour of the eight chapters of *Fratelli Tutti*, let me now sum up what I think has been the reception of the encyclical globally. Unless I have missed it, the reception in Zambia has been very quiet.

5. Reception of *Fratelli Tutti* so Far

Anna Rowlands, a British theologian invited to help present the document at the Vatican, told *Catholic News Service* that the text's "golden thread" is about discerning "what gives life" and "helps everyone to develop their full potential and flourish." Commenting on the *Fratelli Tutti*'s chapter two, a stranger on the road in particular, says, "When people ask, 'Who is my neighbour?' often what they really want to know is "Who is not my neighbour?" or "Who can I legitimately say is not my responsibility." In contrast, she says the teaching in the document "helps everyone to develop their full potential and flourish."[10]

The Czechoslovakian-born Canadian Cardinal, Jesuit Michael Czerny, put it this way, "You could take a distance from the encyclical and say, 'The Pope is trying to get us to recognize that all these people are our brothers and sisters.' But it's more than that. What he's saying is, 'You've got to be a brother and sister to everyone who needs us.' The category isn't out there; the category is here. Our human family and our common home needs me to be brother to the people who need me and needs you to be sister to these people."[11]

Samuel Gregg is less enthusiastic, calling *Fratelli Tutti* a "familiar mixture of dubious claims, strawmen, and genuine insights."[12] Samuel Gregg's critique of the Pope's economic message is blinkered and misses the point of an encyclical. "Also, insufficient — and, alas, this has characterised Francis' pontificate from its very beginning — is *Fratelli Tutti*'s treatment of economic questions," he argues, "It seems that, no matter how many people (not all of whom can be characterised as fiscal conservatives) highlight the economic caricatures that roam throughout Francis' documents, a pontificate which prides itself on its commitment to dialogue just isn't interested in a serious conversation about economic issues outside a very limited circle."[13] This article begs to differ because it understands an encyclical's purpose as exhortative. The Pope is not writing as an economist — he is no Amartya Sen — but a theologian and a pastor.

Larry Chapp, retired professor of theology at DeSales University in Pennsylvania, is more guarded but as he confesses, "Those who know me well understand that I am not generally a fan of Pope Francis, who was elected to reform the Curia (so we are told) but has failed miserably so far in that regard. He has also appointed to high office individuals who seem like old guard, unreconstructed, post Vatican II liberals — which is a bad thing in my view."[14] Having read the encyclical several times, I see no evidence of "Pope Francis' encyclical" suffering "in places with the kind of ambiguities this papacy has all too often engaged in. But it is not, despite what some critics claim, in any way 'heretical' or even 'dangerous.'"[15] I am not sure what's so wrong with his "post Vatican II liberals." And if you are Donald Trump, an encyclical that smells of socialism may well be "heretical" or even "dangerous."

As is to be expected, Carlo Maria Viganò's reaction has been the most vitriolic or malicious. Here is part of his reaction, first in Italian, followed by my translation in square brackets. "Ad una lettura cursoria del testo dell'enciclica *Fratelli tutti* si sarebbe indotti a credere che essa sia stata scritta da un massone, non dal Vicario di Cristo. Tutto quanto vi è contenuto è ispirato ad un vago deismo e ad un filantropismo che non ha nulla di cattolico: *Nonne et ethnici hoc faciunt? Non fanno così anche i pagani?* (Mt 5.47)"[16] [At a cursory reading of the text of the encyclical *Fratelli Tutti*, one would be led to believe that it was written by a Mason, not by the Vicar of Christ. Everything in it is inspired by a vague deism and a philanthropism that has nothing Catholic in it: *Nonne et ethnici hoc faciunt*? Do not even the pagans do the same? (Mt 5.47)]. His conclusion is: "Questa Enciclica costituisce il manifesto ideologico di Bergoglio — la sua *Professio fidei massonicae* — e la sua candidatura alla presidenza della Religione Universale, ancella del Nuovo Ordine Mondiale. Tanta attestazione di subalternità[17] al pensiero mainstream gli potrà forse valere il plauso dei nemici di Dio, ma conferma l'inesorabile abbandono della missione evangelizzatrice della Chiesa. D'altra parte, l'abbiamo già udito: 'Il proselitismo è una solenne sciocchezza'"[18] [This Encyclical constitutes Bergoglio's ideological manifesto — his *Professio fidei massonicae* — and his candidacy for the presidency of Universal Religion, handmaid of the New World Order. Such attestation of subalternity[19] to mainstream thought may perhaps be worth the applause of the enemies of God, but it confirms the inexorable abandonment of the evangelising mission of the Church. On the other hand, we have already heard it: 'Proselytism is solemn nonsense'].

Proselytism, solemn nonsense? Did Pope Francis really say that? I am afraid he did and I think he meant it, when he spoke to the founder of Italian newspaper, *La Repubblica*, Eugenio Scalfari. Proselytism wreaks of forced conversions and is everything that evangelisation is not. Pope Francis was right not to touch Proselytism with a badge pole. This is how Eugenio Scalfari reports part of the encounter. "The Pope comes in and shakes my hand, and we sit down. The Pope smiles and says: 'Some of my colleagues who know you told me that you will try to convert me.' It's a joke, I tell him. My friends think it is you who wants to convert me. He smiles again and replies: 'Proselytism is solemn nonsense, it makes no sense. We need to get to know each other, listen to each other and improve our knowledge of the world around us. Sometime after our meeting I want to arrange another one because new ideas are born and I discover new needs. This is important: to get to know people, listen, expand the circle of ideas. The world is crisscrossed by roads that come closer together and move apart, but the important thing is that they lead towards the Good."[20] But it was Eugenio Scalfaro's conclusion that ties this interview with the insights of *Fratelli Tutti*, "We shake hands and he stands with his two fingers raised in a blessing. I wave to him from the window. This is Pope Francis. If the Church becomes as you think and wish it to be, an epoch will have changed [*Se la Chiesa diventerà come lui la pensa e la vuole sarà cambiata un'epoca*]."[21] If the world listens to *Fratelli Tutti*, or as my friend Josephine Shamwana-Lungu told me recently, adopts "the spirit of *Fratelli Tutti*,"[22] surely, "it will be an epochal change."[23] But before that happens, there will need to be "new bottles for new wine" or "new wine into fresh wineskins" (Mark 2.22 *NRSV*) as the Palestinian Rabbi once put it.

6. How *Fratelli Tutti* is challenging us as Members of CLC

From what we have discussed so far, I think the challenge of *Fratelli Tutti* is obvious. As a biblical exegete by training, it would be remiss of me if I did not use the Bible to distil the message of *Fratelli Tutti*, after the Pope himself does so in several places in the encyclical. I will choose a rather unexpected passage: Cain and Abel.

> "[8] Cain said to his brother Abel, 'Let us go out to the field.' And when they were in the field, Cain rose up against his brother Abel and killed him. [9] Then the LORD said to Cain, 'Where is your brother Abel?' He said, 'I do not know;

am I my brother's keeper?' [10] And the LORD said, 'What have you done? Listen; your brother's blood is crying out to me from the ground! [11] And now you are cursed from the ground, which has opened its mouth to receive your brother's blood from your hand. [12] When you till the ground, it will no longer yield to you its strength; you will be a fugitive and a wanderer on the earth.' [13] Cain said to the LORD, 'My punishment is greater than I can bear! [14] Today you have driven me away from the soil, and I shall be hidden from your face; I shall be a fugitive and a wanderer on the earth, and anyone who meets me may kill me.' [15] Then the LORD said to him, 'Not so! Whoever kills Cain will suffer a sevenfold vengeance.' And the LORD put a mark on Cain, so that no one who came upon him would kill him. [16] Then Cain went away from the presence of the LORD, and settled in the land of Nod east of Eden" (Gen 4.8–16 *NRSV*).

In short, the challenge of *Fratelli Tutti* for us can be summed up as follows: to be our brothers' and sisters' keepers through fraternity and social friendship in our families, neighbourhoods and workplaces. In the words of Pope Francis, so that "we can contribute to the rebirth of a universal aspiration to fraternity" (*Fratelli Tutti* 2020: par 8). Is this Utopian? Of course it is. We are not there yet but that is where we are heading. *Fratelli Tutti*, written as the Pope says, when "the Covid-19 pandemic unexpectedly erupted, exposing our false securities" (*Fratelli Tutti* 2020: par 8) should be our wake-up call. As the Christian ballad by Richard Gillard puts it in the first and last stanzas, "Let me be your servant. Let me be as Christ to you. Pray that I may have the grace to let you be my servant too."

Brother let me be your servant	I will weep when you are weeping
Let me be as Christ to you	When you laugh I'll laugh with you
Pray that I may have the grace	I will share your joy and sorrow
To let you be my servant too	Till we've seen this journey through
We are pilgrims on a journey	When we sing to God in heaven
We are brothers on the road	We shall find such harmony
We are here to help each other	Born of all we've known together
Walk the mile and bear the load	Of Christ's love and agony
I will hold the Christ light for you	Brother let me be your servant
In the night-time of your fear	Let me be as Christ to you
I will hold my hand out to you	Pray that I may have the grace
Speak the peace you long to hear	To let you be my servant too.

Conclusion: Afterlife of *Fratelli Tutti*.

This paper aimed at interpreting and appropriate the message of fraternity and social friendship found in *Fratelli Tutti*. The number of Papal Encyclicals since the modern era is staggering. From the papacy of Pope Benedict XIV (1740–1758), to the papacy of Pope Francis, it is estimated that 299 encyclicals have been churned in the modern era. Pope Leo XIII (1878–1903) holds the record with 85 encyclicals in a papal reign of 25 years, 5 months and 1 day (the third longest reign in modern history). What their impact has been is probably the subject of doctoral theses in pontifical universities throughout the world. Initially, it was up to bishops and episcopal conferences, as it is pretty much today, what to do with these encyclicals. Because of the lack of theological literacy among the laity, encyclicals never quite reached the ordinary Christian in the pew. I fear that this may be the way of *Fratelli Tutti* if we do not do anything about it. That is why this Zoom conference is important and is something of a first — organised by lay people and delivered by a lay person. It should challenge us to go back to our families, neighbourhoods, parishes, Small Christian Communities, country, continent and even planet to ask, "What does *Fratelli Tutti* mean for my family, neighbourhood, parish, Small Christian Community, country, continent and even planet?"

It remains for me to say a big thank you to you all for your interest and attention. Let's go back to our parishes and communities imbued with "the Spirit of *Fratelli Tutti*" and as the Jesuits would say, "*Ad majórem Dei glóriam* [For the greater glory of God].

References

Arteaga, Manuel Martínez (2020), Editorial, *Progressio* [Number 1, 2020]

Chapp, Larry (9 October 2020), *"Fratelli Tutti* and its critics," *The Catholic World Report*, https://www.catholicworldreport.com/2020/10/09/fratelli-tutti-and-its-critics/ (Accessed on 14.10.2020)

Christian Life Community (2020), "Christian Life Community (CLC)," http://www.cvx-clc.net/l-en/aboutUs.html (Accessed on 28.11.2020)

Gregg, Samuel (10 October 2020), *"Fratelli Tutti* is a familiar mixture of dubious claims, strawmen, genuine insights," *The Catholic World Report*, https://www.catholicworldreport.com/2020/10/05/fratelli-tutti-is-a-mixture-of-dubious-claims-strawmen-genuine-insights/ (Accessed on 11.10.2020)

Hinfelaar, Hugo (1994), *Bemba-Speaking Women of Zambia in a Century of Religious Change (1892–1992)*, Leiden, New York, Köln: Brill

Horan, Daniel P (5 September 2020), "The Origin and Context of Pope Francis's Forthcoming Encyclical Title," *Medium*, https://medium.com/@DanielHoran/the-origin-and-context-of-pope-franciss-forthcoming-encyclical-title-984619ab5f01 (Accessed on 06.09.2020)

O'Connell, Gerard (13 October 2020), "Cardinal Czerny on 'Fratelli Tutti:' Pope Francis addresses a world 'on the brink,'" *America Magazine*, https://www.americamagazine.org/faith/2020/10/13/cardinal-czerny-interview-fratelli-tutti-pope-francis-encyclical (Accessed on 14.10.2020)

Opuscula Omnia Sancti Francisci Assisiensis, "Cap. VI: *De imitatione Domini*," http://www.franciscanos.org/esfa/omfra.html#adm (Accessed on 07.09.2020)

Pax Christi (6 October 2020), *"Fratelli Tutti*: A new encyclical," https://paxchristi.org.uk/2020/10/06/fratelli-tutti-a-new-encyclical/ (Accessed on 14.10.2020)

Pope Francis (4 October 2020), Encyclical Letter *Fratelli Tutti* of the Holy Father Francis on Fraternity and Social Friendship, http://www.vatican.va/content/francesco/en/encyclicals/documents/papafrancesco_20201003_en ciclica-fratelli-tutti.html (Accessed on 04.10.2020)

Pope Francis and Grand Imam Ahmad Al-Tayyeb (2019), "Document on Human Fraternity for World Peace and Living Together," Abu Dhabi (4 February 2019): *L'Osservatore Romano*, 4–5

Sala Stampa della Santa Sede, 5 September 2020, *"Dichiarazione del Direttore della Sala Stampa della Santa Sede, Matteo Bruni, 05.09.2020,"* http://press.vatican.va/content/salastampa/it/bollettino/pubblico/2020/09/05/0443/01017.html (Accessed on 05.09.2020)

Scalfari, Eugenio (1 October 2013), "The Pope: how the Church will change," *La Republicca*, https://www.repubblica.it/cultura/2013/10/01/news/pope_s_conversation_with_scalfari_english-67643118/, accessed on 14.10.2020. The original interview was in Italian, "Papa Francesco a Scalfari: così cambierò la Chiesa," https://www.repubblica.it/cultura/2013/10/01/news/papa_francesco_a_scalfari_cos_cambier_la_chiesa-67630792/ (Accessed on 16.10.2020)

Shamwana-Lungu, Josephine (13 October 2020), telephone conversation

Viganò, Carlo Maria (5 October 2020), "Perché critico l'enciclica *Fratelli Tutti*," *Smart Magazine*, https://www.startmag.it/mondo/perche-critico-enciclica-fratelli-tutti/ (Accessed on 14.10.2020)

Winters, Michael Sean (4 October 2020), "'*Fratelli Tutti*' challenges our country and our Church," *National Catholic Reporter*, https://www.ncronline.org/news/opinion/distinctly-catholic/fratelli-tutti-challenges-our-country-and-our-church (Accessed on 04.10.2020)

About the Author

Tarcisius Mukuka is a biblical exegete by training. His ideal job is research in the Humanities and Social Sciences. He holds a doctorate in Biblical Hermeneutics from the University of Surrey in the United Kingdom. His doctoral dissertation was entitled *Orality as Casualty: Contextual and Postcolonial Analysis of Biblical Hermeneutics in Bembaland* (2014). He is currently a senior lecturer in Religious Studies at Kwame Nkrumah University in Kabwe. He is also President of *Theologians against Violence*, a praxis-oriented think-tank with the immediate aim of contributing to free, fair, transparent and peaceful elections in Zambia; beginning with the 2021 General Elections. His research interests include apocalyptic literature, postcolonialism and the Bible, gender and the Bible, the Bible and Misogyny, religion, politics and power. He is the author of *Spoken Voice/Written Word: Negotiating How We Hear/Read the Bible* (2016) published by Lambert Academic Publishing and *In the Eye of a Very Catholic Storm* (forthcoming), by Crown Arts Publishers.

Publications Available on Catholic Education by the Same Author published by GRIN

Mukuka, Tarcisius (2020), "The Great Controversy Unplugged: Ideology of a Religious Classic," Munich: GRIN Verlag, https://www.grin.com/document/955896

Mukuka, Tarcisius (2020), "On calling anyone 'You Fool.' If Jesus did it, why can't we?" Munich: GRIN Verlag, https://www.grin.com/document/952295

Mukuka, Tarcisius (2020), "Anatomy of an Episcopal Dressing down and Clericalism. A Prince of the Catholic Church and an Ecclesial Irritant," Munich: GRIN Verlag, https://www.grin.com/document/948402

Mukuka, Tarcisius (2020), "Pope Francis on '*Convivencia Civil*' and a Movie called 'Francesco.' Is there a Change in Catholic Church Teaching on Same-Sex Unions?" Munich: GRIN Verlag, https://www.grin.com/document/947939

Mukuka, Tarcisius (2020), "The Great Controversy Unplugged: Ideology of a Religious Classic," Munich: GRIN Verlag, https://www.grin.com/document/955896

I am available for presentations or conferences on the above publications on Catholic Education at Catholic Institutions for a small contribution towards research in Catholic Education.

Dr Tarcisius Mukuka

Kwame Nkrumah University
Department of Religious Studies Education

Endnotes

[1] *Christian Life Community* (2020), "Christian Life Community (CLC)," http://www.cvx-clc.net/l-en/aboutUs.html (Accessed on 28.11.2020)

[2] Manuel Martínez Arteaga (2020), Editorial, *Progressio* [Number 1, 2020], page 1

[3] *Sala Stampa della Santa Sede* (5 September 2020), "*Dichiarazione del Direttore della Sala Stampa della Santa Sede, Matteo Bruni, 05.09.2020,*" http://press.vatican.va/content/salastampa/it/bollettino/pubblico/2020/09/05/0443/01017.html (Accessed on 05.09.2020)

[4] Daniel P. Horan (5 September 2020), "The Origin and Context of Pope Francis's Forthcoming Encyclical Title," *Medium*, https://medium.com/@DanielHoran/the-origin-and-context-of-pope-franciss-forthcoming-encyclical-title-984619ab5f01 (Accessed on 06.09.2020)

[5] *Opuscula Omnia Sancti Francisci Assisiensis* (n.d), "Cap. VI: *De imitatione Domini*," http://www.franciscanos.org/esfa/omfra.html#adm (Accessed on 07.09.2020)

[6] Pope Francis (4 October 2020), Encyclical Letter *Fratelli Tutti* of the Holy Father Francis On Fraternity and Social Friendship, http://www.vatican.va/content/francesco/en/encyclicals/documents/papafrancesco_20201003_enciclica-fratelli-tutti.html (Accessed on 04.10.2020)

[7] Cf. Gal 5.22 *NRSV*, "By contrast, the fruit of the Spirit is love, joy, peace, patience, kindness, generosity, faithfulness." *Agathōsýnē* means inherently good or intrinsic goodness (especially as a unique quality and condition; as relating to believers, it is the goodness that comes from God and showing itself in spiritual and moral excellence. The *NRSV* translates as generosity.

[8] Pope Francis and Grand Imam Ahmad Al-Tayyeb (2019), "Document on Human Fraternity for World Peace and Living Together," Abu Dhabi (4 February 2019): *L'Osservatore Romano*, 4–5 February 2019, p. 6

[9] Michael Sean Winters (4 October 2020), "'*Fratelli Tutti*' challenges our country and our Church," *National Catholic Reporter*, https://www.ncronline.org/news/opinion/distinctly-catholic/fratelli-tutti-challenges-our-country-and-our-church (Accessed on 04.10.2020)

[10] *Pax Christi* (6 October 2020), "*Fratelli Tutti*: A new encyclical," https://paxchristi.org.uk/2020/10/06/fratelli-tutti-a-new-encyclical/ (accessed on 14.10.2020)

[11] Gerard O'Connell (13 October 2020), "Cardinal Czerny on 'Fratelli Tutti:' Pope Francis addresses a world 'on the brink,'" *America Magazine*, https://www.americamagazine.org/faith/2020/10/13/cardinal-czerny-interview-fratelli-tutti-pope-francis-encyclical (Accessed on 14.10.2020)

[12] Samuel Gregg (10 October 2020), "*Fratelli Tutti* is a familiar mixture of dubious claims, strawmen, genuine insights," *The Catholic World Report*, https://www.catholicworldreport.com/2020/10/05/fratelli-tutti-is-a-mixture-of-dubious-claims-strawmen-genuine-insights/ (Accessed on 11.10.2020)

[13] Ibid

[14] Larry Chapp (9 October 2020), "*Fratelli Tutti* and its critics," *The Catholic World Report*, https://www.catholicworldreport.com/2020/10/09/fratelli-tutti-and-its-critics/ (Accessed on 14.10.2020)

[15] Ibid

[16] Carlo Maria Viganò (5 October 2020), "Perché critico l'enciclica *Fratelli Tutti*," *Smart Magazine*, https://www.startmag.it/mondo/perche-critico-enciclica-fratelli-tutti/ (Accessed on 14.10.2020)

[17] Carlo Maria Viganò uses the Italian term *subalternità* [subalternity] in its popularr sense of subordination but in its postcolonial sense it carries the sense of Marxist struggle against hegemonic dominance and is understood positively, especially in its use by Antonio Gramsci. Gayatri Chakravorty Spivak, however, understands it more negatively. As Mieke Verloo writes, "Subaltern as a concept is best understood as related to issues of domination and power, democracy and citizenship, resistance and transformation. According to Gayatri Chakravorty Spivak, subalternity is a position without identity, a position 'where social lines of mobility, being elsewhere, do not permit the formation of a recognisable basis of action' (Spivak 2005: 476)." (Verloo 2016: 1).

[18] Carlo Maria Viganò (5 October 2020), "Perché critico l'enciclica *Fratelli Tutti*," *Smart Magazine*, https://www.startmag.it/mondo/perche-critico-enciclica-fratelli-tutti/ (Accessed on 14.10.2020)

[19] See endnote 17 above.

[20] Eugenio Scalfari (1 October 2013), "The Pope: how the Church will change," *La Republicca*, https://www.repubblica.it/cultura/2013/10/01/news/pope_s_conversation_with_scalfari_english-67643118/, accessed on 14.10.2020. The original interview was in Italian, "Papa Francesco a Scalfari: così cambierò la Chiesa," https://www.repubblica.it/cultura/2013/10/01/news/papa_francesco_a_scalfari_cos_cambier_la_chiesa-67630792/ (Accessed on 16.10.2020)

[21] *Ibid.*

[22] Josephine Shamwana-Lungu (13 October 2020), telephone conversation

[23] Eugenio Scalfari (1 October 2013), "The Pope: how the Church will change," *La Repubblica*, https://www.repubblica.it/cultura/2013/10/01/news/pope_s_conversation_with_scalfari_english-67643118/ (Accessed on 14.10.2020)

YOUR KNOWLEDGE HAS VALUE